Recipe
For Winning
A Guide To Success

Natalia Whyte

Publisher: Natalia Whyte

ISBN 978-976-96374-0-5

Dedication

To MY PRECIOUS son, WinAndre Harrison, and my dear brother, Jevaughn McIntosh—may you strive to be the best at all times.

To my selfless and dedicated friends: Nathan Gardener, Sabrina Spencer, Rhondene Wint, Melanie Thomas, Fabeola Kowlessar, Chelsea Taylor and Sedaine Rubie, may God continue to enrich your lives. You all are a testament that great friends are vital in the accomplishment of one's vision.

To my cheerleaders: Winsome Lawson, Maureen Johnson, Nerisa Webb-Tomlinson, Latisha Forbes, Kasia Burke, Tamica Prosphere, Abigail Cannigan, Moya Whyte, Camesha Walters, Kinesha Hutchson, Nicole Ricketts and Lennovia Clarke, you encourage me to give my best daily.

To all my family, students, and friends who helped me hone this gift that God has blessed me with, thanks for always being attentive during our pep talks that helped to build my confidence.

Contents

Give Thanks!

MY MOTHER WAS the queen of thankfulness, and those principles have been emulated by her children.

I thank God for always stirring my spirit with visions for my life and to everyone who has helped to clarify these visions. I would like to extend my gratitude to all the people who have contributed to this journey and who have made it possible for me to live my purpose.

To my uncles, especially Richard and George, I am grateful to you both for playing the role of father so flawlessly after my father passed away while I was still very young.

To my teachers Winsome Lawson and Maureen Johnson, thank you for adopting plus playing the mother role after God called my mother to rest. I also wish to acknowledge the contribution that many other teachers have made to my development. To everyone else who played the role of parents, I extend sincere thankfulness for your loving kindness and support.

Heartfelt gratitude to my special friends: Sabrina, Rhondene, Miss Lawson, Nathan, and Melanie, who prompted me to complete this book even when I was somewhat tardy in doing so.

To all the co-editors who helped in refining this book, I am indebted to you: Dr. Sabrina Spencer, Rhondene Wint, Hillary Walker and Nathan Gardener; I am also grateful to the main editors, Chelsea Taylor, Fabeola Kowlessar and Rachel Fogg (Fiverr username Readwritesell) who edited the book through microscopic eyes.

Sedaine Rubie, thank you for writing your book. This gave me the wake-up call I needed to write mine. I truly appreciate the help you offered when I needed my book edited, formatted and its cover designed.

To all my mentors whose coaching played a role in the execution of my goals and helped me to quit the excuses: Eric Thomas, Lisa Nichols, Myles Munroe, Les Brown, T.D Jakes, Winsome Lawson and Nicole McLauren- Campbell… A big thank you!

Grandma Rose, thank you for investing in me and instilling principles that I will forever hold on to. I am grateful to everyone, especially Grace Lawson, who prays for me daily. Your prayers sustain me, so thank you.

And posthumously to my mother, Miss Olive: thank you for molding me into the lady I am to today. The values and norms you have taught me I strive daily to instill in my son, WinAndre. Mommy, you pushed me to be better.

To WinAndre, thank you for allowing me the time to write this book.

Preface
Why I Decided To Start
Living My Dreams

BEING FRUSTRATED BY the feeling that I was not unlocking my true potential and reaching my goals, I decided to write this book as a form of self-motivation. While I excelled in some areas of my life, I believed that I was capable of achieving more. I yearned for personal growth and bigger accomplishments. Like most people, I made the same New Year's resolutions year in and year out and never stuck to any of them, and the ones I did were inconsequential. Then, there were life events which finally pushed me to take the actions necessary to unlock, wholly, my full potential and finally achieve those goals that I had been neglecting for so many years. I decided to become an author because I felt it was my purpose in life to inspire others to fulfill their life's purpose and achieve their goals, something I struggled with. Becoming an author, goal number 1…checked!

My friend Abigail and I both weighed over 200lbs in 2012, and we started our weight-loss journey in July of that year. We were both on the same program and purchased identical groceries, and she even cooked the meals for me. However, after a week and half in, I quit, although I was losing the weight. I was not disciplined or consistent enough to stick to the stipulations or 'recipes' of the diet. My friend committed to the weight loss journey and she lost 45 pounds; some six years later, she has been able to keep it off. She was and still is reaping the benefits of consistency, self-motivation and discipline. I, on the other hand, over the years have started and stopped more diets and work-out plans than I am willing to admit. I was not determined or resolute in my thinking, and so I made excuses. The more excuses I made, the bigger the number on the scale became, and then my clothes no longer fit. And every year I had to invest in a new wardrobe. Every year, Abigail, Rhondene and I made a pact to lose weight and work on the healthiest version of ourselves. We would find a program together and commit. Well, they did, but I didn't put in the necessary work. This became apparent in 2018 when at a routine doctor's visit, I weighed 267lbs! Putting on 32lbs in less than 4 months…this was **devastating**. I had gained so much weight that the nurse was unable to calculate my BMI (Body Mass Index) on the chart she had. I knew I had gained weight, although I never considered just how much; but I should have known something was amiss when I stopped taking selfies – because I LOVE taking selfies! I immediately blamed hormones for this rapid weight gained and demanded that test be run to check my thyroid levels. I refused to take responsibility for the weight gained, so we had to find the "real reason," which of course had to be medical. The tests came back, and of course I was healthy.

We tend to blame the following for our lack of success: circumstances, situations and others. What are some of the excuses you tell yourself when you are not winning as you should? Remember, we are ultimately responsible for our own lives. For years, I have blamed stress and my polycystic ovaries for my weight. I blamed the unavailability of fresh produce on my island. I blamed my hectic work schedule. While all of those factors might have played a role in weight gain, I could have taken more control of my lifestyle and eating habits. I was what they call an "emotional eater." I ate when I was happy, sad, stressed, or bored. Oh gosh! I became a compulsive eater. I ate when I couldn't afford to pay my bills. I also used meals as a way of celebrating when a goal was achieved. It was an ongoing cycle.

But I digress, because this is not a weight loss book! However, weight loss is something most, if not all of us can relate to, and it wasn't until I started taking responsibility for my weight gain that I realized I needed to take responsibility for my life, and so I did! Is there anything in your life that you are not taking responsibility for? If you took responsibility, how would your life change?

Becoming an Author

In January 2018, after reading Nicole McLaren-Campbell's book "Make it Count," I asked myself, why not write a book? After all, it was my desire to become a motivational speaker and author. I grappled with the thought but never committed to writing. I was never serious about writing. I started putting together a Chemistry Revision book for the CSEC Chemistry Syllabus, but—much like my weight loss journey—I quit on that too. On one of the weekends while working on the Chemistry book, a high school friend of mine called and we were catching up. I told her about my writing, and she shared that she too was pursuing her dream of being an author. Fast forward to September, when her book was published and mine was still just a dream.

You see, I give up on myself too easily and put my dreams in the parking lot of my life. I took too many undeserved rests. Sometimes on weekends, I felt so tired, and why was I tired? For no real reason except I was tired of being tired, I was tired of being lazy, tired of procrastinating. I became frustrated too with not living up to my own personal expectations.

When Nicole McLaren-Campbell released her second book, my book was still being edited. I became fed up with the lies and excuses I would tell myself for not executing my writing goals. I was happy for Nicole's second book and bought it in a heartbeat, but her accomplishment was a gnawing reminder that potential without work is nothing. Ideas without discipline and execution are just ideas.

I am going to pen my book and lose weight. Why? Because I have everything I need to execute those tasks. I realized that in my immediate circle, I had recipes for weight loss and recipes for being an author. I have friends who have done what I aspire to do and are 'winning at it.' I made a commitment that I am going to show up for Natalia, just like how I show up every day for my son, my students and my friends. I am going to be accountable to myself. I am going to live my dreams and I will not stop until I accomplish it.

I have written my top five goals and I have created a schedule, a vision and roadmap.

I am going to employ strategies to win. I am now thirty, and every day I say to myself that I am winning and take one step towards my goals to ensure that I do win. In the chapter *'Work Ethics,'* you will see the methods I used to write this book.

You may be feeling frustrated and angry with yourself. You may have made countless resolutions and are currently not actively pursuing them. The fact that you are reading this book is an indication that you have not given up on yourself and you should not. You may feel discouraged but take heart; speak to yourself with love. As I take you on my life journey, I hope that you will be bold enough to take action and work on yourself. Invest your time and money in yourself to accomplish your God-given purpose and goals.

I wish you all the best on this journey to become a MORE CREATIVE AND INNOVATIVE version of yourself! If I can live my dreams, so can you!

Introduction

I AM A TEACHER who has had both personal and professional success. However, I believe that I was called to be more than just a classroom teacher. I have never said this out loud, but deep down, I want to be an educational consultant with my own science school. I want to coach students on how to live their best lives. I know that is my life's calling. Like many, I want to live my God-given purpose, and like the few, I have decided to start doing so. I intend to produce an authentic book to tell those willing to listen, or rather read, of the struggles I have overcome in my life, the many lessons learnt and the successes I have reaped from what I have sowed. Transitioning from childhood into my early teens, I had all the recipes to accomplish success, and I did. However, in my twenties, I lost my enthusiasm to pursue my goals. In this book, I will give you the tools I used in my pre-teens to achieve those past successes and the ones I am currently employing to attain my present goals.

I believe that God created all of us with the tools we need to succeed and accomplish anything we set our minds to. He gave us those tools and we have used them appropriately to walk, talk and feed ourselves. We have been able to motivate and elevate ourselves and achieve so many other things. Many of us feel trapped and unsuccessful in life. Why? We forgot the tools and techniques that we had used to achieve success in the past. By feeling trapped, we continue to sink into a hole and struggle to climb out.

You must write down your recipe and keep it as your reminder. Every good chef needs a cook book!

I had a student who, when she was in first year of college, called me to assist her with an assignment. It was a two-minutes lesson teaching a moral. She chose to teach to never judge people by their appearance. She felt as though she wasn't fully equipped, and she really wanted to score well on it. While assisting her, I had to critique a voice recording she'd sent. I highlighted her weaknesses and gave her tips to improve her piece. She was very receptive and practiced daily until she got it down to the 'T.' On the day of the presentation, she nailed it and scored 100%. I congratulated her and I told her to reflect on the steps she applied in completing her assignment. We then evaluated the techniques she employed and listed the pros. The pros were: she started the assignment early, got help from an expert and practiced and accepted positive criticism. I told her to convert our conversation into a journal entry. This could serve as a reference point for the future when she feels like she is overwhelmed or on the brink of failure. Her journal entry will serve as a winning recipe for class presentations in the future. Have you ever excelled at something and were very proud of your accomplishment? Did you write down your recipe? Well, what are you waiting for? Think back to an event where you were successful and write down the recipe you used to triumph.

What if you detailed your accomplishments and the steps you took in attaining them? Wouldn't reviewing them make you more confident to achieve more? You would be unstoppable, be more self-assured, and procrastinate less. Those journal entries would become a road map that you can use to re-chart your journey to success. You see, along the way, we lose sight of the winners we are. We allow self-doubt, fear, criticism, and bad company to cripple us and ruin our opportunities to achieve those desired goals. Instead, we should use our previous successes to propel us to achieve bigger and better goals.

As I wrote this book, I reflected on my past; I reminded myself of the **champion** I AM and used this as motivation to finally remove my dream from my life's parking lot. It also serves as a guide to aid others who want to execute their own dreams and be successful.

This book is what I am using to accomplish one of my goals while I rekindle the fire.

Purpose

I am made by the master designer,
Created to do a specific task;
I use my talents, gifts, abilities and personality
In carrying out my job and ultimately enriching the
lives of others.

ALL MANUFACTURERS AND innovators design their products for a specific purpose. The washing machine cleans clothes, the car transport us from one place to another. God, the greatest inventor, created all of us and fashioned us in His likeness—for a specific purpose.

You Have Been Created for a Reason

You were not created to be average, mediocre, or a copy of someone else. You were designed in life to do a task that you alone can do. You are a masterpiece, created by God with your own unique personality, DNA and character; you are an original. The task that you were created to do is just as special as you are. God made us to be a gift to others! You are a gift! Your purpose is personal and unique.

For years, I asked the question why I was created. I asked God and my friends about the reason I was made. My adopted mother, Miss Lawson told me that my purpose was wrapped in my talents, skills and personality and that I must utilize them to enrich the lives of those I come in contact with. If you feel lost or unsure of your purpose, there is no shame in talking to your family and friends and getting their opinion on what they think your true purpose is. Sometimes others are at a better vantage point to inform us of our talents, skills and personality and how they impact their lives. What are some of the things that you are good at and that others may say you are very good at doing? Is it rearranging a house, painting, singing, graphic designing or selling? How often do you do those skills? Make a list of the things you do exceptionally well in the space below.

_____

_____

_____

_____

_____

God made every human being different and each of us holds a gift. Your gift is something that you are good at. He blessed you with this gift to bless others. Myles Munroe (Munroe, 2018) says in his YouTube video, "How To Discover & Release Your Gift To Impact The World," that people go to a mango tree because of the delicious mangoes (gifts) it bears and so too people will gravitate to us because of our gifts. He also says that your gift makes you valuable to others. What are your gifts? How are you using them to help others?

_____

_____

_____

_____

_____

It took me awhile to identify my purpose and I could not comprehend it at first, but after a while, I finally assumed my purpose when I focused on gifts (my strengths) and used them to enrich the lives of others. I have the ability to stand out from others in a room filled with a multiplicity of talents, skills and traits. This could be due to my height, effervescent personality or smile. People have no difficulty remembering something I did or said years later, after only one encounter. I have used my personality to bring cheer in the classroom and staffroom. My current principal introduces me to others as the school's "vibes master," and I have been used multiple times to chair gatherings.

In my teaching career, I have also realized that I was good at motivating and inspiring my students to look beyond their situation and strive always for excellence. At the end of my second year of teaching, I recognized that my motivational quotes and talks resonated with my students and they would write notes after the final examination expressing gratitude for all the encouragement and strength they got from such talks. I began sharing my quotes on Instagram on my @ prettymotivates and @prettywinning social media pages (don't be shy, give me a follow; you won't regret it). My friends would also tell me that the birthday text messages or voice notes they received from me always stood out and encouraged them to celebrate their lives and to strive for better. Are you any clearer now at figuring out your talents and skills and how they can add value to others?

I am also good at writing poems and prayers. I have used this gift to write poems to enhance my science lessons, as well as writing poems for Westwood High School's 135th anniversary and Marjorie Basden High School's 50th anniversary as an ode to the schools achievements, and these were performed at the school's anniversary events. I have written many prayers in my prayer journal and prayers for my students. For the prayers I have shared, everyone loved them. A friend of mine went through my prayer journal and came across a prayer I wrote in 2006 after my mother passed away. It captivated her and she encouraged me to publish them.

I strongly believe that my purpose will continue to unfold as I put myself in various situations to use my gifts and talents. Each time I use my skills is another opportunity to refine them so I can continue to improve. When developing a new dish, every time it is being prepared is an opportunity to improve the dish to meet the cook's expectation.

Guides to Finding Your Purpose

1. Be patient with yourself!

2. Take an inventory of your skills, talent, passions and personality traits.

3. Then, identify and maximize on the things that you are great at and improve on the things that need strengthening.

4. Seize every opportunity to showcase your strength.

It is then and only then that you will be living your God-given purpose using your God-given talents.

On this journey, I have appreciated that we can learn from each and every person because everyone has a unique recipe. My son has reminded me that as children, being naive of the judgments of this world, we were once very eager to display our strengths. He takes pleasure in showing everyone who visits our house his trophy for first place in track and field, and he calls his grandmother to tell her every new thing he does. If we maintain that enthusiasm and show others our skills and utilize them in helping others, our lives will be more enriching and happier.

Every chef has delicious recipes that can be whipped up easily. Your easy recipes are the things you do effortlessly, employing your gifts for the benefits of others. One of the easiest recipes for me to serve is talking to others and brightening up their days. What are yours?

_____

_____

_____

_____

_____

Always seek out ways to use your gifts and talents! This book is a self-help book, so I put my motivational skills at work. I have utilized my poetry at the beginning of each chapter and end with a prayer I have written.

Prayer

Lord, I thank you for creating all of us differently.

Thank you for gifting us with talents, skills and unique personalities so that we can add value to others.

Help us to utilize our creativity, talents, skills and passion so that we can live the life you have intended for us to live.

Amen

Chapter 2
Vision

Our gut feeling, heart's
passion, skills and personality speak.
They instruct us on the things we should do,
and if we listen too,
those ideas create an image,
therefore, forming our vision.

Retrain Your Ideology of Work

WE ALL HAVE desires about what we want to achieve in life to be successful. The idea that was sold to us is that in order to be successful, we must achieve an abundance of material things. So as children, we aspired to be homeowners, travel the world, buy fancy cars and fly in jets. We were trained, or rather indoctrinated, into getting a job, any job, in order to achieve these material possessions which will give us the social standing we crave.

There is nothing condemnatory about getting a job; in fact, it is admirable. After all, I have one... I am a teacher. But sometimes, jobs limit us, and after years of doing the same thing we feel stuck, paralyzed, and trapped. We work as if we are on autopilot and not *really* living. Each day, we ask ourselves, is this really what I should be doing? At times we find that we are even afraid to ask ourselves the question because we are coping, paying bills, and barely surviving; more importantly, we are afraid of the unknown and refuse to take a leap of faith to do what we want to do. It's like eating the same dishes daily. Over time, it loses it flavor.

There is an old adage that states, 'do what you love and you'll never work a day in your life.' If you find a way to do what you love and get paid, then gathering the money for your dream house, car and vacations would be easy. We were not trained to look at our uniqueness, differing personality traits, strengths and passions to see how we can merge them to become the person we were designed to be and to do the job God intended for us. We are often told who or what we are and we accept it without any reservation. Think about what you can do to merge your personality, strengths, passion and uniqueness to create an income and make some notes.

_____

_____

_____

_____

_____

How Do You Decide What You are Supposed to be Doing?

We all have this feeling as if someone or something is tugging on our insides. When it tugs us, we get an idea or thought of what we should be doing. The feeling fills us up with this excitement and gives us an adrenaline rush. This is the guide to your life's vision. Our excitement lasts for a minute or so and then it disappears. When those moments resurface, write them down. Those moments are calls from life, steering you to the path you should be traversing. What does your call from life sound or look like? The excitement you experience is a glimpse of the joy and pleasure that you will experience once you start to live that call. These experiences will help you to figure out what exactly you should be doing with your life. Write them down each time you get one of those tugs.

Describe, in as much detail as you can, what you think you should

be doing. This is your starting point in establishing your vision(s) for your life. Later, with thought, you can refine it.

Return to this space and jot down your tugs here.

_____

_____

_____

_____

_____

The first time I recognized this pull, I was about ten or eleven years old. It happened while I was on a weekend trip to see my godmother. She bore three daughters. I was impressed with them, especially two who attended Westwood High School. I too wanted to be a student of this prestigious high school. I felt the tug every time they spoke of their experiences at the school. I felt I was supposed to be at that school. I got excited just listening to them recalling their experiences and I could imagine myself there engaging in the activities being described. I began to imagine myself sitting in the dining room at supper, playing on the quadrangle and attending the parties in the auditorium. The zeal exhibited by these young women somehow awoke a great desire in me, which I used to form my vision; the feeling I got from their feeling of contentment was indescribable.

Your Vision is Your Blueprint

When you enter the kitchen to prepare a meal, you subconsciously have the end product in mind. Your thoughts are then geared on gathering your ingredients. Then, you focus on getting the ingredients together and later use them to create the dish you desire. Similarly, before building your dream house, you must be clear about how you want it to look and the features it must have. A conversation with the architect will help your clarify your vision and develop a blueprint. The contractors will then work on making that vision a reality. But it all starts with the 'end in mind' vision. A line from the Jamaican National Anthem says, "Give us vision lest we perish." We need purpose and direction in life; having a clear vision and solid work plan gets you to where you want to go.

What are your visions for the next 12 months of your life?

_____

_____

_____

_____

_____

Your vision is like your destination on a road trip. When embarking on a journey, we know ultimately where we are going, what the purpose of being at that place is and the routes to take. We know the time we should get there, especially if it is something important like a job interview or checking in at the airport for a flight. Your complete vision must have the same features: what you want to achieve, the things you need to do to achieve it, the sacrifices you will have to make and the deadline to achieve these goals.

Selecting a high school in Jamaica is just a tough as choosing the right college in America. Students start a curriculum in fourth grade geared towards matriculating into a high school, and then at sixth grade, they sit Grade Six Achievement Examination (GSAT). Students will select the top five high schools of their choice and—based on their performance in GSAT—the Ministry of Education will place them at a school. I decided from fifth grade the high school I would attend. I was going to attend Westwood High School, an all-girls boarding school located in the hills of Trelawny, Jamaica.

In visualizing your goals, you should know how accomplishing these goals will make you feel and the exact changes that will take place in your life; this is crucial. I imagined myself in the Westwood uniform with glimmering gold pin, navy blue tunic with white blouse and straw hat trimmed with a blue and gold band. I felt the pride in wearing my hat. I never knew how the campus looked, but I had imagined myself there several times interacting with my soon to be friends. Attending Westwood was all I could think and speak of during my last year of Primary School. I studied diligently and learned from the mistakes I made in my practice examinations so that I would not repeat those errors again. I was not perturbed either that none of my friends shared my interest in going to Westwood, as it was **my dream**. Your visions are always personal and sometime they pull you away from your friends and current environment in order to achieve them. You will have to make a lot of sacrifices to get your goals, and I had no problem parting with friends. I worked relentlessly to accomplish my goals. I attained a 94% average, which landed me at my dream school.

Are you clear about what you want to be doing and a specific time in which it should happen? If you close your eyes, can you see it? Can you feel the thrills and joys that you will experience when your vision becomes a reality? If your vision is not vivid, spend some time and adjust the lens of your imagination until you have 20/20 sight on that which you want in your life. Replay this vision daily as a reminder of your goals.

Attending the boarding school at the tender age of twelve proved to be quite demanding for a few of my peers; they had difficulties adjusting to the new environment and lifestyle in which they were now placed. For me, this was a walk in the park. I was fine. I was where I manifested myself. I was where I worked and envisioned myself to be and so I never cried; I was too happy living my dream. I had imagined it so many times, and in that moment, it felt surreal to be living the dream.

As a student, I fell in love with teaching. My teachers were great and I admired something in all of them. I wanted to merge all their strengths and be the best teacher I could be. And I aspired and dreamt again to return to work with some of the best professionals in teaching.

My family, friends, classmates and lecturers all knew I wanted to return to my alma mater to serve the students, since I spoke of it so often. I envisioned myself there, and after University, I landed my first teaching job at…you guessed it, Westwood High School! I was elated!

Law of Attraction

At that time in my life, I knew nothing about the law of attraction, nothing about creating a vision board, but I knew a clear vision, being focused, and having determination are vital in creating and achieving what you want in your life I envisioned myself producing this book and I worked daily on making it a reality. The law of attraction, by my own interpretation, is "calling into existence the things you focus on continually, consciously or subconsciously." As you focus on it, you will be inspired daily to take action to get one step closer to your goals. You can also attract bad things too, so be careful what you focus on. Visions will be manifested if you know how to visualize.

How Do You Focus on Your Vision / Purpose?

1. **Vision boarding.** A vision board can be done quarterly, annually or once in a lifetime. This depicts images of how you aspire to live your life and the things you wish to achieve. In making your vision a reality, you can choose images of how your life is going to be. So if you want to lose weight, you can put a picture of someone with your ideal body type or a picture of a fitter you or of healthy foods and exercises. If you want to be a speaker, you can put a picture of someone speaking in front of an audience. If you want to be restaurateur, you can put pictures of a full restaurant, different recipes, chefs, etc. I'm sure you get the idea. Insert quotes also that will stir you to take action to ensure your vision becomes the reality you want to live.

   After making your vision board, place it where you can see it daily. Do not be afraid if others see it. I wanted to be a writer, but I struggled to understand the intricacies of the English language.

Not a good combination if your dream is to be an author. But as I reflected on my past successes, I reminded myself that having a clear vision is important. I created my vision board. I refused to let my poor grammar stop me, so I wrote and got my friends to help, hence the reason for so many coeditors.

2. **Write them down.** Write down the life you want as if you have it. Dreams must be written down as if they have already been achieved. Be very specific: "I improved my grades by 10% this semester," "I paid off 50% of my debt in nine months," "In 2022 I paid the opening and closing fee for my dream home," "I am a sought after web page designer." You get the idea. Write down your goals here.

_____

_____

_____

_____

_____

You can choose to make an audio recording of what you have written and play it whenever you are not near your list.

Review Those Visions Daily

How you choose to represent your vision is a personal choice that is appropriate for you. The key, though, is that you review your visions daily to keep them alive. As you get up, anytime during the course of the day, and before you go to bed.

Take Action
Your Vision Is a Road Map

A clear vision for your life can be a very difficult task to conceptualize, but once it is well defined, you become unstoppable. The next step is to devise a strong *work ethic* to match your vision. Your dream is now a goal because it has a timeline. Break your goals into small pieces that you must achieve monthly, then weekly and daily. Lao Tzu says, "Great acts are made up of small deeds." Be consistent daily and do the small tasks to win big later. You have to be very clear about the things you want and hold tight to your vision.

Some people's desires are just dreams. They lack the drive and self-discipline to work to make them a reality. The key to living any vision is to envision you accomplishing it and a strong sense of purpose to attain it.

You may be saying to yourself that you have started out on your path to accomplish your goals and have been unsuccessful so many times. According to Eric Thomas in his video, "What's Your Why?" (Thomas, 2018) you need to have enough fuel to get to where you want to go. Your fuel is the 'why.' Why must **you** lose the weight? Why do **you** need a car? Your whys will push you when you cannot push yourself. Your 'why' will drive you to your destination. Write down your goals and your whys for attaining them. Pull out that list when you're feeling demotivated or off track and keep going.

Goals	Why

Eliminate Distractions

Your goals are your destination. On your journey to get anywhere, there are some roads that you will have to avoid in order to reach your destination. There are sacrifices that you will have to make in your life in order to achieve what you want. Depending on your goals, you may have to give up things like friends, partying, shopping, and desserts. Nicole McLaren-Campbell says, "You must pay a price." What will you need to give up when pursuing your vision and goals? Do you need to give up shopping in order to secure the down payment on your house? Must you give up partying on the weekends to learn a new skill for your business? Assess your lifestyle and see the things you need to put aside so that you can have more time to spend on being a more successful you.

Goals	Sacrifice

Be Flexible

On your journey, roads will be blocked and detours will arise because of unforeseen circumstances. Would you cancel an appointment with the surgeon because you encounter traffic or road work and have to detour? No! You pause, assess the situation and select a new route. It may take more time to reach your destination, but you will get there. Our paths to accomplishing our goals may change, but the destination remains the same.

Prayer

Lord, thank you master creator,
for planting visions in my spirit.

Give me wisdom to clarify and fine tune
the visions so I can have a 20/20 perspective of the life that you have
called me to live.

Give me directions on how to pursue these visions
and help to keep my eyes fixed on you and
the visions that you have for my life.

Fill me with creativity, provide me with
opportunities to grow so I may be equipped
with the right skills to grow and thrive.

Give me motivation and inspiration to
chart my visions in such a way that people can
see you in me. Surround me with people
who will influence me and fuel me on my journey to become the
masterpiece you designed me to be.

Amen

Chapter 3
Your Work Ethic Must Match the Vision!

Your vision is now a goal.
It is clear as crystal,
getting it
your main objective.
Be your boss—give yourself deadlines, rewards, keep
meetings,
Motivate yourself, sacrifice your time,
Move enthusiastically from task to task until you
shout out-
I did it!
I mastered myself and unlocked my vision.
My purpose is clearer now.

WE ARE ALL privileged to have an equal 86,400 seconds every day. How you invest this time will determine if you live your dreams, someone else's dreams, or your worst nightmare.

Many people want to become wealthy, but they refuse to save, invest, or even indulge in activities to educate themselves about financial matters. In no reality can you maintain the same behavior yet expect change. Whatever you want to accomplish will take hard work, discipline and perseverance, and that's the cold, hard truth.

Map Out the Journey to Your Goal

Every recipe has a method which is a step-by-step sequence of how to combine the ingredients in preparing your dish. Your recipe to winning will require a similar approach. Select one of your goals and think about what you will have to do to ensure that your goal is actualized. Think about everything you need to do to achieve this goal. Think about it in chronological order and write these down.

GOAL:

_____

_____

_____

_____

_____

Draw a flight of stairs and place your goal at the top. Rewrite what you had in chronological order, starting from the bottom of the stairs with your first step until you get to the top. This will give you a visual representation of what you would like to achieve, where you are currently and how far you are from achieving your goals. You will see my staircase to becoming an author. Take pleasure in recording the progress you have made as you go along. Divide each task into daily, weekly, monthly, and even yearly goals. '

Recipe For Winning

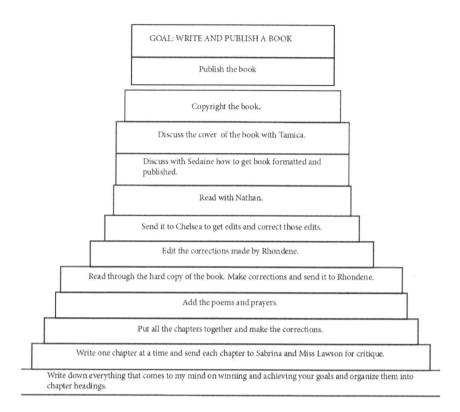

GOAL: WRITE AND PUBLISH A BOOK

Publish the book

Copyright the book.

Discuss the cover of the book with Tamica.

Discuss with Sedaine how to get book formatted and published.

Read with Nathan.

Send it to Chelsea to get edits and correct those edits.

Edit the corrections made by Rhondene.

Read through the hard copy of the book. Make corrections and send it to Rhondene.

Add the poems and prayers.

Put all the chapters together and make the corrections.

Write one chapter at a time and send each chapter to Sabrina and Miss Lawson for critique.

Write down everything that comes to my mind on winning and achieving your goals and organize them into chapter headings.

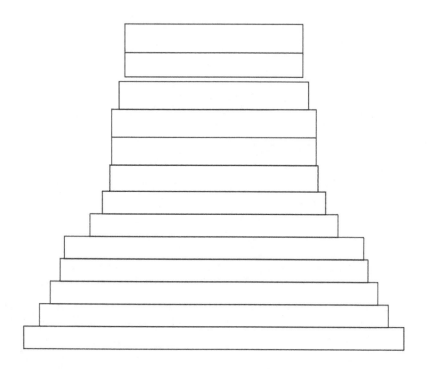

Create your own staircase here. You may not have all the steps but work with basic ones that come to your mind. Add steps as you progress towards your goals.

Get Disciplined

You have to be serious about what you want and be willing to invest the time. The Oxford Dictionary defines discipline as "to train oneself to do something in a controlled and habitual way." As soon as you set your daily task, be diligent about doing it. You may choose a specific time of day to do your goal-directed tasks. It will be hard at first to commit to the task, but you can conquer this by setting alarms and reminders to get it done. Work at it until you become a professional at starting and completing all tasks in designated time slots. Remember, "Practice makes perfect and perfect practice brings perfection," and that it takes twenty-one days to form a habit. The pleasure you will get from ticking off the tasks activates the highest reward system for your brain, as well as the treats and trips you make to reward yourself at each milestone. Conversely, if tasks aren't completed, then take no pleasure in leisure.

So, if you have not been exercising self-discipline and investing your time and energy into creating a better you, then it's safe to assume you are already satisfied with where you are in life and there is no need for you to read any further. But if you are, like most people, not satisfied with where you are currently with your visions, then adopt the motto of 'working today for the life and lifestyle I want for tomorrow.' If you do not become disciplined, then your dreams will remain just that, dreams! You have to be deliberate in your actions in order to be successful. Lack of self-discipline causes the abortion of your dreams, preventing your goals from reaching their full-term. Lack of self-discipline is an act of self-sabotage.

What are some of things you need to get disciplined about? You may be feeling overwhelmed thinking it is a lot of things, but write them down. Do not feel pressured by the length of the list. Approach the list systematically. How? Organize the list by priority, since you cannot successfully work on everything at once. Everyone starts out in January tackling every resolution at once. This is not sustainable, so they quit soon after because they tried to do too much at once and became overwhelmed. I have been there, and that is why I was never successfully able to complete my New Year's resolutions until I changed how I approached them. What did I do? Perhaps you are familiar with the question, "How do you eat an elephant?" Answer: "One bite at a time!" Work on one thing at a time. Take one month to work on the most important task on your list. Take on one new habit a month, and at the end of the year you would have mastered twelve new attitudes.

Be Consistent

While writing this book, my son woke me up at 4 a.m. one morning to use the bathroom. He called out to me telling me that floor was flooded. In an attempt to find the source of the problem, I had to follow the direction of the flowing water. I found the source—I was the culprit. I did laundry the day before and the hose for the manual washer was partially screwed on, allowing water to drip. One drop of water consistently dripping for several hours flooded my entire kitchen, living room, bathroom and bedroom. It took me two hours to remove all the water. Unconsciously, while sweeping out the water, I contemplated about the power of consistency—the power that transformed a single drop into a flood.

Consistency is the key to living any dream and fulfilling any task. It is hard to be consistent—believe me, I have struggled with this my entire life—but here's what has worked for me. Break up those big goals into smaller, manageable tasks, and make those tasks a daily priority. Do not proceed to another task until you have completed one task. Fostering the habit of task completion is the weapon for success. These small tasks eventually add up to the successful completion of your bigger goal.

Keep working to live your vision! Constantly work at it. "We demand that our spouses, friends and boss be consistent, yet we do not do this for ourselves," is a favorite expression used by Eric Thomas. A mother training a child on habit has to be consistent in her actions. I recall teaching WinAndre, my son, to greet everyone when entering a room. Whenever he entered a room, I was vigilant in watching his actions to see if he was achieving the objectives. One evening, he burst through the door and did not greet anyone. I sent him outside to return again and again until he greeted everyone. It took daily consistent reviews and praise, but he has finally accomplished this goal.

In writing this book, I had to commit my evenings to writing. At first it was hard trying to fit it into my routine, having to sit for hours. But after weeks of doing so, writing became the routine.

Quit Complaining

My father died when I was six, my brother when I was ten, and my mother when I was at age eighteen. I could have held a pity party and lived my life complaining that life is hard and I do not know what to do. Instead, I rose to meet those challenges head on. I brushed myself off and made something happen for myself. I took responsibility for my life. I tried not to complain about what I did not have, but rather focused on what I still had. To support myself through college and to subsidize the money I got from my uncles, I started teaching Chemistry on the weekends and I sold costume jewelry on campus. I made it happen for me despite what life threw at me.

It's easy to complain about the things that are not going right in your life; there is always something or someone to blame. Even so, your excuses will not make your dreams come true, add value to your life, increase the money in your account or add to your assets. Instead, it subtracts from your life, robbing you of its joys.

I learnt early in life that everyone's life is not perfect. Everyone has issues and problems, and it is the overcoming of these obstacles that makes our story unique and makes us resilient, competent and better individuals. I therefore urge you, do not complain about the circumstances in your life. But if you must complain, at least come up with a solution. There is always one! If you want to be the best, you have to execute. Eric Thomas constantly stressed that everyone wants to be a beast until it time to do what the beast does. Give yourself pep talks, and if that doesn't work, remind yourself why you need to accomplish your goals.

Embrace Failure

On your mission to accomplish your goals, you will experience the highs of triumph and lows of failure. Learn to celebrate your success. Commend yourself on completing your task. There are going to be moments when you are stuck. It will appear as though nothing is working although you are trying everything. You are going to fail and fail several times. Winston Churchill stressed that, "Success consists of going from failure to failure without loss of enthusiasm." The key to triumph over failures is learning your lessons. Learn the lessons, step back and realign yourself, find new strategies and try again until you accomplish your goals.

Although I was very good at Mathematics during my high school years, I struggled with Physics and often failed so badly that I cried. The teacher asked me before sending up my predicted grades for the Caribbean Secondary Examination Council (CSEC) Physics paper what grade I thought I would get. Confidently, I told her grade 1, and she wrote it down. I worked those last few months on making that goal a reality. With the assistance of my teacher, principal and the strongest students in the class, we worked assiduously day in and day out to get my grade 1 in Physics. Despite those efforts, I failed the physics "Mock Exam" a week before the finals. I was depressed, embarrassed, shattered and dejected, but I was resolute and determined that I would conquer that Physics exam. I remembered my goal, I stood steadfast, I did not dwell on the failure, I practiced daily, got continued help, studied, scored my grade 1, went to college and, today, I am a high school Physics teacher.

Prayer

Thank you for giving my vision.

Give me self-discipline to do what I must to accomplish
my goals and vision.

Give me patience to persevere through adversities.

Teach me wisdom so I can learn from my mistakes.

Fill me with courage to do the work necessary.

Inspire me daily to work on my vision,

grant me tenacity to continue when I feel like striking out.

Lord, help me to remain focused continually on my tasks until I have
faithfully accomplished them.

Remind me, oh God, that you are right here with me
every step of the way.

Amen

Chapter 4
Water the Grass You Want to Grow

Continuous learning is a must.
Concentrate on your skills,
Work on developing new ones,
Invest in your learning,
And watch as you bloom into an expert.

HAVE YOU EVER been on a long journey and you noticed that some lawns are more luscious while others are eyesores? Some home and business owners have taken pride in their surroundings and have invested time and resources into their landscape. They have watered, fertilized and groomed their plants, making their gardens and lawns attractive. Their well-manicured lawns and gardens are so captivating that along the way, we stop to admire them and even take some photographs.

Why Do Some People Excel, and Others Do Not?

You may know people with identical skillsets. Do you notice that some people excel and achieve more from cultivation of their skills than the rest? Why? Those who succeed are extremely passionate and have invested time and energy into the development of their skill or skills. They put in the effort, consistency and discipline that they need to hone their skill or talent. They have watered their gardens. They have sacrificed and done the work so their gardens can be attractive. Other people may not recognize their talents or have not taken the time necessary to develop the talents they have identified. Some people have not dug deep within themselves to release the gift that God has given them.

I have had students who have been able to fully contour and create art on their faces with make-up and are also exceptional at creating that perfect look. Why are they good? They are good because they have watered their makeup garden. They invest their time watching makeup tutorials on YouTube, they have invested their money to purchase the tools and products they needed to become successful makeup artists. They get ecstatic to use foundation, pencils, pallets, powder and brushes to create a flawless masterpiece that will accentuate beauty. They watered that skill.

No recipe is perfected all at once. It takes experimenting, time and practice to perfect it. What skills have you developed by watering?

_____

_____

_____

_____

_____

Some people are naturally good at something and require little or no training to get results. However, we are capable of learning new things once we put some effort into watering that skill we need to acquire. I always thought I was incapable of combing hair, however, I decided that I would watch some YouTube videos on relaxing hair and I successfully relaxed my hair twice. My colleagues were shocked that I did not visit the hairdresser to do this. When my friend, Nathan, encounters any issue with his car, he watches YouTube videos on the causes and learns how to fix them. He has invested in purchasing tools and parts in order to competently fix his car. Nathan has saved thousands of dollars fixing his own car as well as his friends' cars. He has even taught himself how to fix phones, laptops and other electronic devices.

Learning a new skill helps to foster self-confidence, builds character, improves your resume and helps you to save money.

Always Stay Interested

Nathan says it takes 99% interest and 1% effort to excel in anything you do. He believes that once you are interested, you will be on a path, constantly yearning to find out more about it. The one percent will be executing the knowledge you have gained.

As a young teacher, I was always passionate about the teaching and learning of Chemistry, and so I watered that passion by investing in books and reading journals as well as CSEC Chemistry reports in order to detect weaknesses that students have on specific topics. From my research, I have designed tools and strategies to prevent these students from making those errors. I spent time studying past papers and organized them topically to help the students answer examination questions. I reached out to other more experienced teachers who would be able to facilitate my passion. My mentor, Mr. Gayle, gave me lesson plans and trained me in the marking of laboratory exercises. I have had a 99.2% success rate so far in the CSEC Chemistry Examinations, and I have had students in the top ten in Chemistry for Jamaica. This is a testament to the success you can reap by sowing an interest and watering it daily.

The grass is not greener on the other side! The grass is greener where it is watered. What skills and talents do you need to water or perhaps cultivate? Is it baking, writing, speaking, acting, programming, coding, animation, massaging or marketing? Whatever you are interested in, you have to become hungry to find more information and give yourself time to master the art to develop the expertise required.

What skills do you need to develop? What can you do to develop those skills?

_____

_____

_____

_____

_____

Ways to Water Your Garden

What are some other ways to water your skill sets to keep the lawns in your life properly manicured?

1. Find a mentor in your field of interest and find out more about what they did and are currently doing.

2. Read books and blogs and subscribe to YouTube channels to be more informed and keep current.

3. Take an online class. There are several websites that offer free classes in almost every field.

Learning is Continuous

I am always interested in upgrading myself, improving my ability to teach science and helping students be the best. I may not have gone back to school, but I try to remain up to date on current theories and research that I believe will help students. I engage with colleagues via various social media platform to learn about new pedagogies from teachers around the globe. Why do I do this? So I can be relevant and keep up with what is trending in science education. Ultimately, I want to have a 100% pass rate with students ranking number 1 within the Caribbean. Whatever you do, never stop learning; keep current in your field. Doctors and nurses have to undergo continuous professional training annually in order to renew their licenses, and you should be no different.

There are so many people who will boast about the number of years of experience that they have in their field, but sometimes those many years of experience is just one year of experience being repeated multiple times. I am not saying you should reinvent the wheel, but I am urging you to be creative and innovative to experiment so you can evolve.

Whatever field you serve, you can keep ahead by investing money and time into learning a new skillset. Very often people start a job being the best candidate, but after being there for over a year, they are the same person. Nothing has changed. They have made themselves obsolete by not watering their talent or skills. They have not read any articles, taken any classes or made any improvements in themselves, thus remaining stagnant. What are some trainings you need to get to be better at your current job?

_____

_____

_____

_____

_____

Pay Attention to What You Water

Practice makes perfect. Whatever you repeat daily will become a lifestyle. So, try not to water lateness, procrastination, lies, self-doubt, alcoholism, worrying about things going wrong, over eating, smoking, etc.

We also tend to water the negatives in our lives, by 'practicing' those habits much more often than necessary with little or no benefit to our lives. For a long time I have watered procrastination, doubts and fears, and so they crippled and hindered me from being the author and the motivational speaker I aspired to be. Regardless of my aspirations, night after night I allowed myself to get lost in my Facebook and Instagram pages. I watered laziness, and so I had to make a concerted effort to water my writing skills, and in doing so, I started reading more. In order to water my motivational speaking skills, I watched Les Brown, Eric Thomas on YouTube and Nicole McLaren-Campbell on Instagram. To put what I learnt into practice, I always began my classes with a mini motivational pep talk for my students.

Prayer

Lord, thank you for my skills and talents. Plant me
in places that I will water them.
Provide me with the right mentors.
Give me courage always to bloom where I am planted.
Help me, Lord, not to be distracted by others and worry about the
skills and talents I don't have.
Let me concentrate on my talents and invest my time and effort to
improve them.
Amen

Chapter 5
Find Your Inner Child

Children are filled with promise and are optimistic
about their future,
determined to find out about their world,
resolute to keep trying.
Perseverance and praise keep them going until the
task is completed.

As a child growing up, I was stubborn and relentless in getting my way. The more they told me not to do something, the more I did it. My brother and I were sent to the shop one afternoon, and in an effort to remember what to purchase, we started singing the names of the items. Our father called out to us, telling us to stop, yet we went on our journey and I sang even louder hugging, my brother as we went along to get the items. On returning, our father did not spare the rod for being stubborn. I never forgot it. That was the first time my father gave us a beating. Regardless of being 'disobedient,' I knew my stubborn attitude would one day help me to accomplish my goals.

Never Give Up

Like most mothers, I watched my son accomplish his milestone of walking. He tried and tried after falling many times, but he did not quit. Today, he is beyond walking; he is running around. I can hardly keep up. A child practices and practices, never stopping until he or she gets it, whether it's walking, talking, coloring within the lines. Daniel Coyle writes in his book *The Talent Code*, "Practice doesn't make perfect. Practice makes myelin, and myelin makes perfect." Myelin is the substance needed for brain cell growth and is developed each time we practice. The best chef practices often to perfect their skills, and you must practice if you are going to win.

Have you ever started anything then abandoned it because you just could not get it? You gave up too quickly. You did not allow the myelin to develop. Sometimes we give up too quickly on ourselves; we need to continue until we accomplish our desires instead of quitting in the middle of our developmental stage. Sometimes we even unknowingly quit in the last lap, within arm's reach of our success. It took persistence and resilience for Thomas Edison to create the first light bulb. Can you imagine how hard our lives would be without that invention? You are a genius waiting to happen in your field. Learn from your mistakes and try not to repeat them and, each time you fail, cry if you must. But get up, assess the reason for the fail and keep moving. Practice, practice, and never stop honing your art until another person starts asking how it is done. Practice until you become the coach.

Is there anything you need to start practicing?

_____

_____

_____

_____

_____

The perfect barrel of wine needs time to properly ferment and age to become that expensive bottle of wine served. If the winemaker gave up on the barrel too quickly, you would not have that perfect bottle of red wine to pair with your steak dinner.

Never Take No for An Answer

Children do not like taking no for an answer. They will ask, annoy, negotiate with you until you meet a reasonable compromise. Remember in high school when you wanted to hang out with your friends, you would try your hardest to coax your parents into sending you?

Do you recall how I shared that I wanted to attend Westwood? That was not my mother's plan, as she could not afford the tuition. However, after pleading and begging, she said that I could select the school, but I had to select it for my last choice. When my aunt arrived at the school to fill out the GSAT entrance form, I told a lie. I do not condone lying to get what you want, but at the time, I thought it was necessary. I told her my mother said that Westwood should be my first choice. After passing the examination with terrific grades, my mother was shocked that the government sent me to my 'last choice.' Little did she know that I was going to be attending my first choice.

Remember growing up how there were several things that you wanted to do, and you were so headstrong in doing it no matter what anyone told you? You did not care about anyone's permission. So why now, as an adult, are you sitting, waiting on your spouse, boss and friend to give you permission to pursue your purpose and accomplish your goals? Find your inner child, go and chase your dreams.

Knock on doors of opportunity until one opens and if that doesn't happen, pry the door open until you accomplish what you want and get what you want from life. **You don't need anyone's permission to live your dreams. Just go for it!**

Do you need something to push you further to achieve your goals?

Have you heard no from someone? How can you navigate past that no to get to your goal?

Never Forget Your Manners!

Growing up, especially in Jamaica, good manners were instilled at home and at school. I was trained to smile and greet people. Stand every time a teacher entered the classroom. Be appreciative and express gratitude to others for their kind gestures. Be respectful to others, their ideas and property. In my experience as a teacher, I've realized that good manners seem to be outdated and not practiced much in this generation. You will interact with people in all spheres of life, so do not forget your manners. Remember, treat others as you would like to be treated—the golden rule.

Good manners also mean expressing gratitude to those who help us along our journey. I would like to thank everyone who has contributed to my life thus far. Whether it was good advice, prayers, hugs, money, favors, or support, I appreciate what you have done for me.

Are there any people who you need to acknowledge for the role they have played in your life? You can give them a call, send a text, write an email or even send a voice note.

_____

_____

_____

_____

_____

Stay True to Who You Are

In pursuit of your goals and living your purpose, be true to who you are. Never lose your integrity to climb the ladder of success. Never lose your authentic self.

Growing up, I always tried to be the same person at home and at school. My mother had a heart condition, and I could not afford to misbehave or take on another personality at school so she would be called in and be shocked at the Natalia she would be introduced to there.

When I changed jobs, I brought my attitude of success with me. People insisted that I adapt to the culture, but I had a feeling that meant that I must change and metamorphosis into something that I was not. I refused to be mediocre and accept sub-standard work. I motivate and inspire my students to pursue excellence in all they do; I continue to build critical thinking. I practice what I preach.

We advertise who we are daily by the way we live and the things we speak about ourselves. Strive daily to ensure that your action and words are the same. If your boss should review his interview notes, are you the passionate and hardworking employee you advertised? Are you the spouse you told your partner you are? Is the kind of parent you are today that parent you wanted for yourself or the one you aspired to be? Spend some time and see if you have deviated from your authentic self. If you have deviated, why have you? How can you get back to your true self?

_____

_____

_____

_____

_____

Always Find Time To Play

Growing up in Jamaica, this adage was frequently said: "All work and no play makes Jane a dull girl and Jack a dull boy." You must be able to strike the balance between your work and fun. Schedule play time. Always make time for what relaxes you. You have to take timetable breaks during the day while you work, even fifteen minutes to step away from your desk. Listen to your mind and body and take breaks when you are tired. Take care of yourself! Breaks help you to stay physically strong and mentally alert on your journey to living your purpose. Relaxation helps to fuel your creativity. Try also to take weekends off, where possible, to spend time with your family and friends.

Take time and make effort to go on simple vacations. Plan a day trip, a day pass, a cookout, a small tour of your community or country instead of spending all of your life saving for that all-inclusive resort and spa that sometimes never happens.

Remember you are an adult; you do not need permission from anyone to live your purpose and to achieve your goals. Be relentless and fearless and never take no for an answer. Never give up on yourself. Practice until you become the master.

Prayer

Dear Lord, thank you that I am your child created by you.

Your words say, unless I become like little children,
I will never enter your kingdom.

It is true also that unless I find my inner child,
I will never be the success you want me to be.

Give me curiosity to investigate the best way to
use my gifts in the service of others.

Give me persistence and patient to carry out the task I must in order
to fulfill the purpose for which I was designed. Enable me to find rest
to refuel and recharge myself to be refreshed for your service.

Amen

Chapter 6
You are Your Own Competition

You are a masterpiece,
unlike any other
Your only competition is you:
your skills, your abilities, your talents.
Strive daily to be better than who you were yesterday.

After assessing my first report card in grade seven, my mother taught me never to limit myself. My mother was proud of my overall performance; she commended me, and after singing praises, she began to analyze my subject performance. My highest and lowest grades stood out. I had scored 95% in Mathematics and 59% in Spanish. She gently inquired why the Spanish grade was so low. I began to explain to her it was the first time I was being exposed to Spanish and it was hard. She said it's the first time you are doing this kind of Mathematics, so the same 'Talia' who did that could do better in Spanish. The school had a forty/sixty system, coursework to exam respectively. She pointed out that my examination grade for Mathematics was 59/60 and it was unacceptable that the overall grade in Spanish was my examination performance in Mathematics. She encouraged me to do better in Spanish and told me that I should apply the same technique that I used in Mathematics. I took her advice, and the next term I scored over 80% in Spanish.

In Myles Munroe's book *Maximise Your Potential,* he stated, "True success is what you have done compared to what you could have done." Some people measure their success not on what they have done compared to their own capability but what they have done compared to others. My favorite line from the Desiderata is, "If you compare yourself with others, you may become vain or bitter, for always there will be greater and lesser persons than yourself." If you have never read the Desiderata, I recommend you do so after you finish reading my book.

Are you maximizing your potential? Are you capable of doing more than you are currently doing?

_____

_____

_____

_____

_____

Check Your Progress

My mother had the ritual of comparing every new report card with the previous cards and comparing my performance. She believed that my grades should also be improving. It did not matter if I was first place in a particular subject area; the mandate was simply to improve every term, even by a single percentage. She would start her presentation by saying, "Talia, you should be getting better." It would annoy me at the time, but I later realized she was right. I should have been improving. As a teacher, I have adopted her strategy and have my students plotting their performance after each assessment on a graph so they can visualize their progress or lack thereof in my class.

When you take your success seriously, you will strive daily to improve yourself so that you can metamorphosis into the expert you want to be. You will constantly push yourself to achieve exponential growth. Daily, your goal must be to push yourself beyond where you were yesterday. This is a principle body builders and gym fanatics use daily to transform their bodies and keep going regardless of the pain.

Do Not Compare Your Journey to Anyone Else's

Every child develops differently. Some are able to walk at seven months while other walk after a year and six months, but ultimately, all physically healthy babies will walk. Once you are exerting the force necessary to improve yourself daily, you will achieve your desired success. So do not feel pressured or frustrated that you are not going as fast as others.

It is said comparison is the thief of joy. Growing up we did not like to be compared to our sibling or our neighbors' children. It would hurt us and robbed us of our joy. So why do we compare ourselves to others now as adults?

Consider the following situation:

My uncle finally acquired his own house at age 50. For years, people would ask him why he was still paying rent. They would advise him to get a loan for a house and use the rent money to pay his mortgage. He was resolute that he was not going to pay any mortgage. After saving his money for years, he was able to build a six-bedroom, four-bathroom house with kitchen, living and dining areas with all modern amenities in just fourteen months. His house is modern and is admired by all who visit it. Soon after this accomplishment, he was able to buy another property which had two houses on it. Many people believe fifty is too late to acquire property, but my uncle did while his friends are currently paying huge mortgages. He had his own dream, vision, methodology and was resolute in his conviction and although some would consider it late, he was able to acquire two properties by age 52.

Everyone defines success differently. Many of us hate going to high school reunions; we are afraid to showcase who we are now because we feel insecure and inadequate. DO NOT MAKE PEOPLE USE THEIR DEFINITION OF SUCCESS TO MAKE YOU BELIEVE

YOU ARE UNSUCCESSFUL. Be cautious to live according to your terms and not be rushed by other peoples' timelines for your life.

What is your definition of success? What are your terms?

_____

_____

_____

_____

_____

There Are Different Routes to Success

There are various modes of land transportation that can get you to your destination. Likewise, in reaching your desired goals, there are several different routes you can take.

In Jamaica, a trained graduate teacher holds a teacher training diploma as well a bachelor's degree. I desired to be a teacher for many years, so I spent three years studying at a teachers' college and graduated with a diploma in teaching instead of a degree. Since ultimately my goal was to graduate as a trained teacher, I went to the University of the West Indies Mona Campus to accomplish this goal. My peers from high school attended either sixth form or community college for two years and then later enrolled into university for the degree program for a further three years. Based on the nature of the courses I took at college, we all wound up in second year at the same university, where we graduated together. We took different routes to get there but we all achieved the same goal: a degree.

Based on your situation and abilities, you may have to create your own route to achieve your goals. Success doesn't follow a straight line. What works for others may not work for you. So you need to assess what is an effective way to achieve your goals based on your current job, family life, personal responsibilities and finances. Map out your own journey to success and travel it until you have achieved your goals.

Stop the Social Media Craze

People disproportionately highlight the best of their lives on social media. You may see the cars, mansions, vacations, or successful businesses but can't see the journey they took to achieve this. Stop studying their material possessions and instead study their journey. How many times did they fail and were resolute that they would not quit? They are not overnight successes. Amazon was not always a trillion dollar business with hundreds of hubs scattered all over the world! It started in a garage. Successful people have done their work. They have planned, failed, cried, reassessed and repeated that process until they are now the sought-after entrepreneurs, speakers, designers and marketers who we admire today.

Don't get distracted by what looks like overnight successes; they are not! It takes experts time to dominate their fields. They had to work hard, sacrificed their time, and often delayed gratification in their pursuit of excellent. Work on yourself and your business. Practice, practice, practice until people ask you how it is done.

Research a successful person in your field and write down some of the hardships she/he has encountered and overcome.

_____

_____

_____

_____

_____

Be patient with yourself, strive daily to improve your skillset, chart your own path and do not get distracted by another person's journey.

Prayer

Dear Lord, forgive us for not utilizing the talents
you have placed in us; forgive us for killing
the dreams you have planted in our souls.

Forgive us, always, for comparing ourselves to others because you
created us to be originals. Help us, oh Lord, to tap into our true
beings and build on what you have given us to work with. Grant us
with patience, patience to deal with ourselves.

Amen

Chapter 7
Let No Obstacles Stop You!

Disappointments will come,
opportunities missed,
you may hear no, no and no again.
Do not be deterred:
keep focus and do not lose enthusiasm,
be bold and have faith in yourself and your abilities,
and never be too quick to give up.
A back door or a window of opportunity may open
up for you.

THE JOURNEY TO living your purpose will not be smooth sailing. You will encounter rough seas, broken sails, storms, noxious smells, enormous turbulence, sea monsters and fear of the water. Franklin D. Roosevelt coined "a smooth sea never made a skilled sailor." It's these delays, setbacks and challenges that will push you to rely on your faith in God and yourself. It will add color to your story and make your success sweeter. These bittersweet encounters will build your character, resilience and perseverance. Lisa Nichol proposed that in everything we experience, there is a lesson. What blocked my path became the path. Some obstacles were at times opportunities that were disguised as obstacles. Therefore, we shouldn't give up too early but ask ourselves, what can I learn from this?

Perseverance Is Key

Quitting is the easy way out because living your purpose and manifesting your vision takes patience and a persistent attitude. Obstacles and detours surely await you along your journey, but I urge that you do not see them as roadblocks but instead as signposts leading to a better, more resilient you. Show up, press on and follow up until you accomplish your desires.

This story below shows why you must exercise faith and determination along your journey to winning. I applied to the Mico University College to major in Mathematics but ended up switching to Science. The government at the time had a scholarship for students who wanted to be Mathematics and Science teachers, and I had an interest in those subjects and the scholarship was the only way for me to get a tertiary education. I lost both my father and my older brother when I was young and my mother had spent all her life savings on health care for them. My mother, at the time, was terminally ill herself. My grandmother was the one who funded my high school education, and at her age, she could not afford to send me to University. Therefore, this was my only shot, and as you can imagine, I went for it.

Most of my family members were encouraging me to go and get a job after leaving high school, but I watched them all working and never feeling satisfied because they had no qualifications so they were underpaid and could barely afford to support themselves and their family. That was not going to be my life.

I had sat the entrance examination in March 2006 for the Mico University College but I was not successful, hence I was not called for an interview. I was a bit disappointed, but I knew I did well in the CXC examinations, which are the ultimate prerequisite for admission to the University, so I was confident I would get in. I had faith in myself, my abilities, and all the work I had put in. Still hopeful that I was going to University, I took my CXC results in after they were released. I worked hard to earn grade ones in Mathematics, Physics and Chemistry. Deep down, I felt confident that they would accept me, even though I failed the entrance examination. On the day I got my results, I took it to the University, where orientation was already on its way. The lady who was collecting the documents took the paper from my hand and proceeded to copy it; however, feeling as though this could be my only shot, I politely asked her to take a look at it. While looking at it, she seemed impressed and gave me a favorable response, saying that she would call.

You must actively and fearlessly pursue your success. Go for it! Not hearing from her by midday, I called her the next day and asked what the next step was. She said I should just be patient and wait for a call. Positive I was going to attend "Mico," I returned the following day. This time, I went for the uniform design and the voucher to pay for the medical assessment. The lady in the main office was confused and questioned why I needed those documents when, to her knowledge, I did not even do the interview for full acceptance to the University. I politely told her that my classes would begin the next week and I needed to have my uniforms ready for that time. The lady said she admired my determination and she would take me straight to the faculty of Science office to do my interview. Although not properly attired for an interview, I followed her. She explained to the lecturers that I was not formally dressed but I was determined to start school and asked them to conduct the interview on the spot, to which they agreed. The interview went well, and I started school the following Monday fully attired in the Mico University uniform.

In life, you can choose to sit and wait on others to decide your fate for you, or you can decide and take action for yourself. I learnt early that I must be relentless in the pursuit of my goals. You have to be hungry for success and work hard to accomplish your goals. In accomplishing my goals, it meant I must knock on doors for opportunity or even bang on them, if I must.

I got the scholarship and graduated top Science student in 2009, becoming the first member of my maternal family to graduate from college. Special thanks to everyone who contributed to my journey at the Mico University College.

Your Potential Attracts Investors

At the end of college, I travelled to the United States of America for work to secure my first semester school fee for University, despite being offered a Government-funded scholarship. I had to pay my first semester's fees. However, problems always find a way to present themselves. After returning for school, I had experienced difficulty registering at the

University, so the payment for my tuition fees could not get processed. After sorting out the registration, I was finally given a voucher to pay for the semester; however, I found out that a member of my household stole my tuition fee. I was enraged. I had worked so hard during the summer, working double shifts, fainted a few times and even had to go to hospital just to have my hard-earned money stolen. I fell into despair, and to make matters worse, I had no redress for my stolen money.

By that time in September all the schools had already filled their vacancies, so I could not find a job as a teacher. I started my University studies with no way of paying; I had no family member who was interested in loaning me that kind of money. I thought of quitting and locating some students to tutor on the weekend to survive.

I decided I was going to seek a loan from my college lecturers. I had two lecturers who always said I was going to be a great teacher and they admired my passion for the sciences and teaching. I called them and explained my dilemma and asked them for a loan. They did not hesitate and loaned me a sum that totaled half of my school fee, which was enough to get the accounting department off my back. Even though I still had half left to pay I went in faith, and like good fortune it worked out. My boyfriend gave me some, my adopted father gave me some, and a high school friend of mine, after getting her first paycheck in France, sent the remainder. There it was, my school fee fully paid. My friends and lecturers saw my passion and always told me I could be the teacher I am today, and they invested in me at a time I needed their investment.

In seeing my potential and feeling my fire, they were willing to give me support to pursue my degree to live my dreams; there are people willing and waiting to do the same for you. Sometimes all you have to do is ask.

At times, you may become frustrated because the people who you think are supposed to help you are not in a position to help. Share your story and sell your passion to those around you and people will support your dreams in the form of cash, loans, gifts, advice and support. Who can you call to assist you today, and what do you want from them?

_____

_____

_____

_____

_____

When setbacks come your way, be creative, exercise faith and do not be quick to quit!

Prayer

Father, ignite passion in me.
Let it blaze so I will be fired up to live my purpose.
Let others see my passion and be motivated and inspired to assist me in anyway necessary to carry out my God-given talent.
Give me drive so that I will continue to chase my dreams and purpose even when I encounter obstacles, setbacks, and disappointments.

Amen

Chapter 8
Speak Life

Beautiful Words of Wisdom Let it Be!

The words we speak have force;
they are magical and shape who we are.
Speak to release such power in your life,
speak growth and positivity.

IF WE SHOULD take a time capsule to return in time to our childhood years, we would realize that we had so much vision for our lives. We believed then that we could conquer the world and acted as such. But along the way we allow people, circumstances and experiences to define us, telling us we can't and that we aren't good enough. Over the years, we allowed these factors to label us, and as a result, placed ourselves in a box made by others, ultimately diminishing our self-worth.

Your Definition Matters Most

You should never allow other people's opinions of you to become the definition of who you are; if you do, you will take on all their negative projections and energy, which will eventually drain your optimism, sucking the life out of your dreams. No one deserves such power in your life except you! It is your life! Do not allow people's negativity to deter you. However, understand that constructive criticism is always welcomed. Learn the difference between someone who wants to make a better you and someone who wants to change who you are and kill your dreams.

My favorite childhood song has always been, "I am a promise." I have always believed that I am a possibility and I have great big bundles of potential, and I am a promise to be anything God wants me to be. Since we are all created to do a task, I am pretty sure we were fully equipped and are more than capable of doing such. God has given you the ability within to win.

So sit, reflect and recapture your thoughts, and control your inner voice. Thoughts form words, words form action and action, habits.

Words Have Power!

Tupac Shakur, a well-renowned rap artist, said, he knew "he was going to be shot" and it was a shooting that killed him. Vybz Kartel, a famous dancehall artist, has a song about his mother coming to visit him behind bars and now, he is serving time. Life and death are in power of the tongue. Choose to speak life, speak words of wisdom, and they will consume you and your life. Speak it until your subconscious believes it. For a very long time, I was unhappy and frustrated about the happenings in my life and kept repeating that I was tired until eventually, all I could feel was being tired. I ended up having to stop professing I was tired and said I am mentally and physically capable of completing the tasks I have to do. The days I felt physically tired, I said to myself that I feel a little exhausted today.

Here is another vivid example of why we shouldn't speak negativity into our life or allow anyone to do the same. In December 2017, I had a lot going on but I wasn't stressed to the point where I couldn't manage; however, I kept repeating, "I am so stressed." This thought eventually overpowered my consciousness to the point where I had to be hospitalized after having severe chest pain. I thought I was having a heart attack. Not surprising that, after visiting the doctor and after a thorough historical and physical examination, the diagnosis was that nothing was wrong. I was just stressed!

Stop speaking ill of your own life! People who believe in the law of attraction say we attract into our lives what we speak and what we are. What are some negatives that you are constantly repeating about or to yourself? Are you seeing how they are shaping your life negatively?

Therefore, let us speak blessing, joy and prosperity in abundance over our life. You can start and end your day with positive affirmations. Write down some positive affirmations you can speak into your life to combat the negatives.

Negatives Previously Said	Positive Affirmation To Combat Negative

Be Kind with Your Words

As children, we all recited, "Sticks and stones may break my bones but words will never hurt me." Let's be honest, how many times has someone said something negative to or about you that has cut your soul so deep that some of these scars feel as if they will never heal? The person speaking harshly to you is oftentimes yourself, and sometimes the way we speak about ourselves we would never dream to speak that way about anyone else. I have a friend who, when she was in grade 8, had a teacher say something horrible to her; some sixteen years later, she is still hurt by those words. Many divorcees are still angered by the harsh words spoken by their spouse some many years after, and some of these same words led to the divorce in the first place. The opposite is also true when we feel inspired and encouraged when positive words are spoken to and about us.

Speak life and blessing over your children's life. Too many parents speak negatively about their children and highlight all the wrong they have done, never commenting on the positives. Let us praise our children and keep the conversation positive so we can foster a positive culture in their lives. For every negative you hear in your life, counteract it with something positive. Peoples' opinions of you should not be your own opinion of yourself. Psychologists say that it takes 16 positive events to counter 1 negative event. So, create a positive space.

Your mind is yours! Take complete control of it. Rewire the way you think and change your path.

At Westwood High School, one year, the school's theme was, 'Positive thoughts, positive feelings, positive experiences.' I loved it! It encouraged the staff and students to change their thoughts to foster positive experiences in school.

Reset your minds and transform your thoughts so your actions can be ultimately transformed and improve the quality of your lives.

Prayer

Loving God, help me to choose words that will edify
and uplift others.
Help me to speak to myself with love.
Help me to forgive those who have spoken negative word in my life
that I replay and hurt me daily.
Help me to focus on the positive words others have spoken over me.
Help me to weed out the negative weeds that are in mind. Help me to
rewire my thinking and to think positively at all times.

Amen

Chapter 9
Keep Good Company

Your friends mold you and shape you daily.
They can push you toward or deter you from
achieving the dream.
Choose people who will help you to be better daily.

As CHILDREN, WE were cautioned to keep friends who would have a positive impact on our life. As a student at Westwood High School, I was cautioned on the ABC of friendship: Avoid Bad Company. You may think that as an adult you have refined your selection of friends, but sadly, this is far from true.

Positive Peer Pressure

Peer pressure has been studied for years, and people tend to see the negative end of peer pressure. If you have the right friends, though, peer pressure can be instrumental in living your purpose and executing your dreams. I remember one year at school we decided to delay issuing report cards from December to January. My colleagues and I decided that instead of relaxing our efforts until January, we would work on the report just as if it was going to be issued in December. Other teachers saw our efforts and followed suit, and in January we were all just reviewing the report cards as the bulk of the work was already done.

If you surround yourself with people who are obsessed with achieving their goals and living their purpose, you will become one of them. If their mission is self-improvement, then professional, personal, emotional, spiritual and financial growth is high on their agenda. Jim Rohn, a popular motivational speaker, says, "You are the average of the five people you spend time with." If your friends have a winning mentality, it will force you to develop the winner mind set as well. Those friends will hold you accountable and will force you to move towards a plan of action. I have friends who will call and check on my goals and review my progress and vice versa. Our conversation is deeper than the news, memes and social media trends. We are there to motivate and inspire each other to live our best lives while achieving goals and meeting deadlines. A few of my friends held me accountable during the writing of this book. I am also a part of a health group where the members hold me accountable to my weight loss goals. Do you have at least one friend who checks in on you and holds you accountable to your goals? Describe that relationship and state how it can be improved.

_____

_____

_____

_____

_____

Do You Need to Change Your Friends?

Friends to avoid:

1. Friends who treats you like a trash can. Their sole purpose is to offload their stress, worries and frustration on you. They are constantly venting and complaining and they never have anything positive to say. After each encounter, you feel depression and despair.

2. Memory boxes. These friends only talk about the past. It's good to reminisce, but if there is hardly any futuristic conversations and they are living in the past, then you may need to distance yourself.

3. Party goers. I am not referring to your friend who is a deejay, party promoter, or bartender. Nor am I referring to friends who can balance partying without jeopardizing their goals. My schoolmate Chelsea, from high school, enjoys partying and she holds two bachelors' degrees and a master's degree from a top-ranked university in the world and many other certifications. I am talking about the person who is constantly partying and then they complain about the life they have. They want to go out to escape their life, so they choose partying instead of taking the necessary actions required to make the change. Choose friends who invest their free time on their skills, family, relationships and goals, as they are actively on a quest to face their imperfection and to improve their quality of living.

4. The constant complainers. There is always a problem with these friends. They are the ones who always have a problem with everyone and everything other than themselves. Those friends have a problem with every solution given.

I am not asking you to discard your friends, I am asking you to take an inventory and make sure your friends are fueling you on your mission to accomplish your goals. You need to ensure also that you are a representation of a good friend.

Choose happy people who are constantly growing and the ones who influence you to be better. Surround yourself with people who value and respect you and your ideas. Have friends who will help you cry when you are down but help you to find solutions to your problems. Remember, you must also be a good friend to others. But start by being a good friend to yourself. Speak kindly to yourself. Listen to your thoughts and speak words of encouragement to yourself. And then, by extension, you will attract positivity and spread the same to your friends, which will become a cycle of happiness and continuous goal attainment.

Prayer

Lord, thank you for the gift of friendship.

Help me, Oh Lord, to find friends who will
guide me to be a better person,

friends who will push me to give my best always and will encourage
me to stay true to your tenets.

Lord, give me friendship like David and Johnathan,

friends who are loyal, trusting, caring and unafraid to speak the bitter
truth I may be unwilling to hear.

Lord, I don't want a lot of friends, but I need few who will make my
journey here on earth easier.

They will support me when I need it and brighten up
my days with laughter.

Remind me daily, dear Jesus, that the most
important friendship I have is yours.

Amen

Chapter 10
Choose Optimism

In a world of financial crisis, broken homes,
it's easy to complain about what is going wrong.
But you can choose to be an optimist,
Focusing on the positives

Change the Way You View Challenges

YOUR BURDENS AND struggles are there for others to see how resilient you are and how much you have overcome to be the beautiful soul you are today. They are not weights made out of lead that you must carry to weigh you down. They are definitely not an excuse you use to justify remaining mediocre. They are not secrets to hold in your heart. Your struggles are trophies highlighting your wins! Your obstacles are like the hurdles in a 100m hurdle race. At the beginning of the race you staggered over them, almost toppling, but you regained your composure and started clearing them. The bad experiences we have in our lives are trophies to remind us that we are winners and champions. Although faced with difficulties and obstacles, you have made it. You keep going even though you faced setbacks and hardships. Display your "trophies"; they commemorate your achievement and your will not to give up. Use them to motivate and inspire others who are also facing adversities or similar daily struggles. People may judge you, but do not worry about them. You know how you struggled and how broken and ripped apart you were. *You are no longer a victim but a victor!* You rose from the rubble of your life and you made it one step closer to what God called you to be.

Disappointments are Appointments

Disappointments are setting you up for something bigger and better. In November 2018, my son was scheduled to have a hernia repair surgery. We reported to the hospital, but we were not admitted because the surgical bed was not working. We rescheduled the surgery for January 2019. In December 2018, I found out he had to do another surgery. Had he done that surgery in November he would have had to do another minor operation again. Because his surgery was delayed to January. he was able to do both at the same time. Delays are going to come in your life. The setbacks and obstacles that you will definitely encounter in your life must be thought of as frameworks for greater things to come. It's human nature to feel bad when something doesn't go as planned, but you have to trust God that all things will work for the good of those who love the Lord. Thank God for the delays you experience and watch as better things unfold that will blow your mind. Lord, thank you for successful surgeries.

Disappointments can be Crossroads/Turning Points

My friend, colleague and housemate Rhondene applied for several graduate schools in order to acquire a master's degree. She had invested her time in filling out the application forms and writing her essays. She spent money on application forms and examination fees. Her dream schools rejected her. She felt disappointed, rejected, angry and frustrated. I remember telling her to cheer up and examine it from a different perspective, that it was not her time for her move yet. My talk did not exactly soothe the situation immediately.

After the initial shock, grief and disappointment, she enhanced her resume. She taught herself computer programming and reapplied a year later. She got accepted to her school of choice but this time to pursue a PhD program in the number one public research university system in the world. The master's degree was her plan, but there was a bigger and better plan in store for her with this acceptance to a PhD program.

Flavor Your Half-Filled Glass of Water

As a science teacher, a glass filled halfway with water is never half empty as gas occupies the other half. It's easy to focus on that which you do not have. I lost my optimism about some issues and my friend Nathan said, "Motivational speakers are positive people. If you are going to win and encourage others to do so, you must be a positive person." Even if the glass is half-full for you, focus on the water you have. Be creative; seize the moment to make the water great. Grab some sugar, sweeten the experience, and you can add your own flavor to it. That way, even if you still see it as half-full, it is flavored to your liking.

Develop the Negatives

Life comes with what we call negatives as well as lots of positives. We place the negatives under a powerful microscope, which increases the magnification and drowns out the positives. As humans, it is quite common to focus on what's going wrong. What if we forgot about the negatives and zoomed in on the positives? Before digital photography, pictures would be taken by using film to take a photograph. The film then underwent chemical treatment and a negative would develop. The negatives would then transform into a beautiful photograph. The negatives produced a positive image that will remain a memory for years to come. In negatives, there is beauty, but you have to train your brain to see the positives in the negatives.

I left from Westwood to take up employment on the Turks and Caicos Island. This was because the salary was way more than I was earning in Jamaica. I was always excited to experience a new culture. Although the income was higher, I felt I traded my life and comfort for money. I missed my family, friends, the Jamaican culture and recreational activities I would do with my son. For the first few months,

I thought that migrating from Jamaica was a bad decision. I did not appreciate the slow pace of the island or the many free hours I had. I saw it as a negative, and for a year I held this view, but I changed my thinking. I told myself I must be viewing this wrong, and with detailed analysis I found the pros to my situation. I found I had more time to: bond with my son, work on my goal staircase and start my online classes, to name a few. My 'free time' was no longer spent moaning about the change of lifestyle but about making decisions to ensure I would win and create the life I wanted for myself and my son. Are there any negative situations in your life you need to develop a positive from? Make a list of these circumstances and the positive outcomes that arise.

_____

_____

_____

_____

_____

Shift Your Focus from the Limes

Imagine getting a succulent, beautiful edible fruit arrangement from a special someone. Would you toss it out because you see a few limes in the arrangement? No! You look beyond the limes. You should concentrate instead on the juicy pineapples, the sweet oranges and the delicious chocolate covered strawberries. You should express gratitude and embrace the thoughtfulness and kindness of your friend. So stop focusing on the limes in your life and celebrate and enjoy the positives. Stop allowing the negatives to rob you of the joys that will bring you happiness.

Stop Focusing on Unaccomplished Resolution

At the end of the year 2018, I reflected on what I have accomplished, and I have done a lot:

1. I went on my first vacation to Dominican Republic with my son, where we had an amazing time.

2. I sent my book to Sabrina and Rhondene for review.

3. I shed 37lbs.

4. I read more books.

5. I found love.

6. I bought some laboratory apparati for my school.

7. I taught physics for the first time, where all my students passed.

Sure, I did not do all I had wanted, but I accomplished so much and for that I am most grateful and very proud of myself. I celebrated my WINNING accomplishments and toasted to making 2019 a greater year. I wrote myself a letter reminding myself that I am a winner. I tucked it in my purse and pull it out on days I need a reminder that I can get it done.

Make a list of things you have accomplished and are proud of throughout your life.

_____

_____

_____

_____

_____

Prayer

Lord, teach me to develop a grateful heart.

Help me to stay positive during adversities.

Teach me to focus on things that are going great in my life.

Let your Holy Spirit quiet my heart when
I become anxious and feel despaired.

Father, when I am disappointed, help me to look to see the
appointment you are setting up.

Teach me to be anxious about nothing.

Let me always celebrate the good in my life and
help me not to let setback keep me negative.

Amen

Chapter 11
Letter to Reader

Dear _____ *(insert your name)*,

I want to remind you that you are a masterpiece created by God to single-handedly do a task that no one else in the world is capable of doing. The sperm that fused with your mother's egg is one in three million (1/3,000,000), so you were a winner before you were even born, and you're a winner now.

It doesn't matter the circumstances in which you were conceived. **You are in God's plan.** God chose you, and it was destined for that viable sperm to meet that mature egg.

You are so special that God knows the number of hairs on your head. You were created in His image and likeness, so the next time you feel insignificant remember you are special, one of a kind. You, my dear _____, are alive for a purpose. You may feel down, pressured, stressed and frustrated with your life and feel as if no matter what you try, it's just not right, and you may feel like throwing in the towel. That's okay! That's a normal part of the motion. Another spectacular motion is to give yourself a second chance and strategize until you get it.

Transformation starts in your mind. So, start by changing your mindset. Change the way you view yourself and your situation. You are not broke; you are currently only paying bills to survive, but money will come in soon. You can change one bad habit each month to kickstart your weight loss journey. You are one interview away from your dream job. You are only one investor away from starting your business. Like many failed experiments, you may only need to change one variable in your approach to reap the results you want.

Keep a journal and track your effort and progress. Scientists keep a log of their experiments and revisit it constantly, trying to reap the results they want; sometimes just tweaking something reaps bigger benefits.

You are constantly changing, and you are the best experiment you will work on, so find what brings you peace, happiness and what fuels you to give 100% on days you feel like giving up. Give yourself room to explore, fail, succeed and—like a child who is learning to walk—cheer yourself on and do not quit until you reap the success you are craving. Practice until people ask you to coach them. Each time you fail, whether it is small or large, correct yourself in love and help yourself to do better next time.

Spend time with yourself; love yourself and care for you just as much as you care for your friends, family, spouse and children.

When negative thoughts creep up on you, silence them or shut them out by counting backwards to 1 from 5 and chant something positive about you. 'I am good at _____.'

Best of luck to you on your journey to achieve greatness and ultimately living your purpose.

Cheers to being a better you and loving yourself for the man/woman you are today, knowing that you are blooming in your purpose.

Love, light and purpose,

Natalia

My prayer for you,

_____.

Lord, thank you that this person invested their time
and money in this book.

May this this book transform their life and may they work to live the
life you have called them to live.

Reveal in them the skills and talents you have
planted and help them to grow.

Give them discipline and perseverance to stay through
to accomplish their goals.

Give them the right mentors and, as they embark
on this journey to living their life calling,

surround them with friends who will help them through this journey.

May they see themselves as the winner you have created them to be
and the winner you see them as.

Allow them to zone out the negative criticism
and learn from positive ones.

Teach them to love themselves as the unique masterpiece they are and
may they stop comparing themselves and their journeys to others.

Give them the confidence and boldness they need.

Give them the right investors and allies they need
to execute their goals.

Amen

The End

Made in the
USA
Lexington, KY